# IPHONE 14 PRO CAMERA:
# BEGINNER'S HANDBOOK

An A-Z guide to help you maximize the use
of the powerful cameras on the iPhone 14
series (14, Pro, and Pro Max): tips and
tricks to take breath taking pictures, and
videos

## Jeremy Lawson

**Table of content**

# Introduction

Having a smartphone is great. Having the new Apple iPhone 14 is even better. A myriad of benefits and innovative upgrades make this flagship device stand out from other smartphones.

Among these several benefits are the impressive camera upgrade from previous iPhone models, brand new display technology and novel safety designs. These make the new Apple iPhone 14 a uniquely crafted masterpiece.

The iPhone 14 features an Always-On display that essentially creates a lowly-lit Lock Screen with the device's wallpaper from which notifications can be easily accessed while consuming just a tiny fraction of its battery.

Making its debut on the iPhone 14 series, the Dynamic Island, which is both a software and hardware innovation, shows device activities alerts, and notifications in one place and can just as easily transform into a tracking and control panel for Music, Lyft rides, etc.

The iPhone 14's camera systems are out of this world. Providing detailed, highly visual and colorful images like that from four pro lenses. Each photo from the iPhone 14 now has 4x more information thanks to the quad pixel sensor. Also, the A16 Bionic powers its new Photonic Engine and analyzes and perfects each pixel with up to 4 trillion operations giving each image an even finer look and more detail and sharpness.

For videos, the iPhone 14 also offers a new Action mode that permits a gimbal-like stabilization for action scenes with the ProRes and Dolby Vision video technology. Professional filmmakers can even benefit from a more powerful Cinematic mode with 4k resolution and 24-fps recordings.

Asides relying on the iPhone 14 for quality picture shots impossible for most film cameras, the novel technological device is also capable of satellite communication with Emergency SOS to help in emergency situations. This new emergency solution makes the iPhone 14 a must-have and genius accessory in emergency situations that can provide critical information necessary for help automatically to emergency services even in remote locations without Wi-Fi and cell service reception.

Coupled with the A16 Bionic chip that is supercharged by nearly 16 billion transistors, making it the fastest chip any smartphone had ever seen, nothing really comes close to the Apple iPhone 14 series. This book takes an in-depth exploratory approach on the features, capabilities and frequent how-to questions of the new iPhone 14.

# Introducing the iPhone 14

## Design of the iPhone 14 Camera

**The new Main camera** has quite a larger $f/1.5$ aperture alongside 1.9 µm pixels that permits video and photo improvements no matter the lighting conditions for each scene while featuring better detail and less noise, motion freezing, sensor-shift optical image stabilization, and faster exposure times.

**For its new front TrueDepth camera** that has a staggering $f/1.9$ aperture, it allows for better low-light performance for videos and photos. When trying out the autofocus for the first time, it has the ability to focus a lot faster in lowly-lit conditions and take group shots from farther away.

**Also featuring a new Action mode** that provides an astonishingly smooth-looking video which adjusts appropriately to significant shakes, vibrations, and motion, even while video is being captured while the action is going on.

**The iPhone 14 Ultra Wide camera**, guarantees a one-of-a-kind view for wider shots, as well as improvements to low-light photos shot with Photonic Engine.

The iPhone 14 also boasts of **an augmented True Tone flash** which is now ten percent brighter and even features better uniformity for a more consistent lighting.

**The Cinematic mode** on the iPhone 14 is now available in 4K at 30 frames per second and 4K at 24 frames per second.

Also offering **End-to-end Dolby Vision HDR**, that is only available on iPhone.

## What's so special about the iPhone 14 Cameras?

An in-depth exposition and detail of the iPhone 14 cameras reveal that the Apple iPhone 14 series' cameras have seen another augmentation yet again for an iPhone series. The two devices in the iPhone 14 series —6.1 inches and 6.7 inches —both have impressive range and camera upgrades that set them apart from other Apple devices.

The iPhone 14 and the 14 plus have a 12MP rear or main camera that boasts of larger pixels and a large sensor while the front camera situated right on the Dynamic Island is a TrueDepth camera which is a new development among Apple iPhones.

With the Ultra-Wide camera that gives one-of-a-kind perspectives and includes a wider range within a single shot, and the Photonic Engine which is essentially an enhanced image pipeline that is responsible for great pictures in low-light conditions, nothing comes close to the iPhone 14 cameras.

## Versatility of the Camera System

The Photonic Engine, for all cameras, has specifically been modified to help shooting in mid to dimly-lit scenes and provide great images. This versatility naturally requires a boosted performance for efficiency, which the Photonic Engine adequately provides for shooting in these mid to dimly-lit scenes. It also provides a 2x performance boost for the TrueDepth Camera, 2x performance boost for the Ultra-Wide camera and a whooping 2.5x for the new Main Camera.

# iPhone 14 Pro Camera Zoom

The iPhone 14 Pro model has three camera lenses which, cumulatively, make up a single camera system, are:

- 13mm at 0.5x with an ultra-wide lens.
- 24mm at 1x with the Main lens.
- 48mm A5 2x with the Main lens.
- 77mm at 3x with a telephoto lens.

From one of the earliest iPhones in the year 2016, the iphone7 plus, dedicated with a 2x lens, to the most renowned smartphone, the iPhone 13 pro model, with a 3x camera lens, the iPhone 14 is said to be the best digital and most convenient device for computational photography.

With the help of the 48MP sensor, which is 65% larger than the iPhone 13 Pro model, the new Main camera has 2x low light improvement for photos, compared to the iPhone 13 pro. It can also capture images with the help of the 12MP ultra-wide camera, at a 3x improvement. This resolves the compromise made with a 2.5x and 3x camera and provides a more brilliant image than any iPhone 2x and 3x lens accessible.

## Tech Specs

The iPhone 14 Pro features a myriad of impressive technical specs that are listed below:

**Body**: The iPhone 14 series have a Stainless-Steel design and a Textured

Matte glass back with a Ceramic Shield front.

**Capacity**: Storage capacities available for both iPhones in the series are:

- 128GB

- 256GB

- 512GB

- 1TB

**Size and Weight**:

The weight and size of the iPhone 14 Pro is:

Width: 2.81 inches (71.5mm)

Height: 5.81 inches (147.5mm)

Depth: 0.31 inch (7.85mm)

Weight: 7.27 ounces (206 grams)

The weight and size of the iPhone 14 Pro Max is:

Width: 3.05 inches (77.6mm)

Height: 6.33 inches (160.7mm)

Depth: 0.31 inch (7.85mm)

Weight: 8.47 ounces (240 grams)

**Splash, Water, and Dust Resistance:**

Both iPhones are rated IP68 under IEC standard 60529 which equates to a maximum depth of 6 meters up to 30 minutes.

**Apple Pay**

Available on both iPhones in the series.

**Safety**

Emergency SOS via satellite

Crash Detection

**Location**

Precision dual-frequency GPS (GPS, GLONASS, Galileo, QZSS, and BeiDou)

Digital compass

Wi-Fi

Cellular

iBeacon microlocation

**Video Calling**

FaceTime video calling over cellular or Wi-Fi

FaceTime HD (1080p) video calling over 5G or Wi-Fi

Share experiences like movies, TV, Music and other apps in a FaceTime call with SharePlay

Screen Sharing

Portrait mode in FaceTime video

Spatial Audio

Voice Isolation and Wide spectrum microphone modes

Optical zoom with rear-facing camera

**Audio Calling**

FaceTime audio

Voice over LTE (VOLTE)

WI-FI calling

Share experiences like movies, TV, Music and other apps in a FaceTime call with SharePlay

Screen Sharing

Spatial Audio

Voice Isolation and Wide spectrum microphone modes

**Audio Playback**

- Supported formats include AAC, MP3, apple Lossless,

FLAC, Dolby Digital Plus, and Dolby Atmos

- Spatial Audio Playback

- User configurable maximum volume limit

**Video Playback**

Supported formats include HEVC, H.264, and ProRes HDR with Dolby Vision, HDR10, and HLG

Up to 4K HDR Airplay for mirroring, photos, and video out to Apple TV (2nd generation or later) or Airplay 2-enabled smart TV

Video mirroring and video out support: Up to 1080p through Lightning Digital AV Adapter and Lightning to AvGA Adapter (adapters sold separately).

**Siri**

Available on both iPhones in the series

# Technical Specs

## Cellular and Wireless

- 5G (sub-GHz and mmWave) with 4x4 MIMO8

- Gigabit LTE with 4x4 MIMO and LAA8

- Wi-Fi 6 (802.11ax) with 2X2 MIMO

- Bluetooth 5.3

- Ultra-Wideband chip for spatial awareness

- NFC with reader mode

- Express Cards with power reserve

## Chip

A16 Bionic Chip

6-core CPU with 2 performance and 4 efficiency cores

5-core GPU

16-core Neural Engine

## iPhone 14 Battery

The iPhone 14 Pro model indisputably has the best battery life to be produced in an iPhone operation.

It provides about 23-hour battery life for video playback, a 20-hour video streaming playback, and provides up to about 75 hours of audio playback, an advancement of the iPhone 13 pro model.

The iPhone 14 pro model is designed with an in-built rechargeable lithium-ion battery. The iPhone Pro Max model, on the other hand, provides about 29-hour battery life for video playback, a 25-hour video streaming playback, and provides up to about 95 hours of audio playback. They offer a charging speed of about 50 percent charge within 30 minutes with a 20W adapter or higher.

It also gives a Qi charging up to 7.5W, a MagSafe charging up to 15W, and also a wide collection of digital sensors which include the Face ID, the high dynamic range gyro, the LiDAR Scanner and so much more.

Other tech features available on the iPhone 14 series include:

- Voice Control

- Zoom

- RTT and YTT support

- Type to Siri

- Siri and Dictation

- Assistive Touch

- Back Tap

- VoiceOver

- Magnifier

- Closed Captions

- Switch Control

- Spoken Content

The iPhones in the 14 series also use eSIM technology and are not compatible with physical SIM cards. Two eSIMs can be active at a time while provisions are available for storing up to 8 eSIMs.

## Design and Display

The iPhone 14 Pro has 6.1 inches (diagonal) of all-screen OLED display. This measurement takes into consideration the rounded corners which are within a standard rectangle. Measuring the screen with the actual rectangle in consideration, it measures 6.12 inches diagonally. The iPhone 14 Pro uses a Super Retina XDR display alongside a 2556x1779 pixel resolution at 460 ppi.

The iPhone 14 Pro Max, on the other hand, has 6.7 inches (diagonal) of all-screen OLED display. This measurement takes into consideration the rounded corners which are within a standard rectangle. Measuring the screen with the actual rectangle in consideration, it measures 6.69 inches diagonally. The iPhone 14 Pro Max uses a Super Retina XDR display alongside 2796x1620-pixel resolution at 460 ppi.

Both iPhones in the series also have the following tech features:

- Dynamic Island

- Always-On Display

- ProMotion technology with adaptive refresh rates up to 120Hz

- HDR display

- True Tone

- Wide color (P3)

- Haptic Touch

- 2,000,000:1 contrast ratio (typical); 1600 nits peak brightness (HDR); 2000 nits peak brightness (outdoor)

- Fingerprints-resistant oleophobic costing

- Support for display of multiple languages and characters.

## iPhone 14 Camera

The iPhone 14 and the 14 plus have a 12MP rear or main camera that boasts of larger pixels and a large sensor while the front camera situated right on the Dynamic Island is a TrueDepth camera which is a new development among Apple iPhones.

## iPhone 14 HDR Feature

The HDR feature or High Dynamic Range is a feature that allows you to take great pictures in high-contrasts scenarios. This feature works by taking several pictures in a quick succession and then blending all of them to reveal more shadow detail and highlight in your pictures.

The HDR feature automatically activates by default once a high-contrast situation is detected. iPhone 12 models and later can record videos in HDR, capturing exact colors and contrast.

## How to use HDR mode on iPhone 14

### Turn Off Automatic HDR

Some iPhone models can manually toggle on or off the HDR feature. To turn off the Automatic HDR,

1. Open Settings,

2. Click on Camera

3. And then select Turn off Smart HDR.

4. Next, from the Camera screen, click on HDR to either turn it on or off.

## How to Keep the non-HDR version of a photo

The HDR version of a picture is typically stored in Photos by default. To keep the non-HDR version of a picture,

1. Open Settings,
2. Click on Camera and then select Keep Normal Photo.

## Turn HDR video on or off

Turning off the HDR feature for video recording is possible for iPhone 12, iPhone 13, and iPhone 14 models. To do this,

1. Open Settings,
2. Click on Camera and then Select Record Video.

From there you can tap Turn off HDR video to stop recording video in Dolby Vision HDR for true-to-life color and contrast.

# About the Apple iPhone 14 Pro Camera

The iPhone 14 Pro features 3 main cameras —the main wide-angle camera, an ultra-wide camera, and a telephoto camera that has 3x optical zoom. The main camera's lens has a wider focal length of 24mm as opposed to the 26mm equivalent on previous iPhone models. This focal length on the iPhone 14 Pro may not be a steep difference from previous models, however, it does include more of the scene in the frame.

Also, with the main camera comes a new and larger 48MP sensor. Larger megapixels do not necessarily mean better photos, however, with the iPhone 14, Apple, via pixel binning guarantees brighter images with less image noise.

Pixel binning is the technique that involves separating the pixels into four groups, then combining the four in each group into one larger pixel.

Also, within the iPhone 14 Pro's Camera system is the Photonic Engine which is Apple's new and enhanced image pipeline. The Photonic Engine functions to protect image details, improve color accuracy and ensure great pictures in low-light conditions.

## Apple iPhone 14 Pro Camera Features

The features with which the iPhone 14 Pro camera is endowed include:

**A pro-camera system:**

Which primarily involves the 48MP camera with a quad-pixel sensor, a focal of about 1.78 aperture with a 24mm. It can also be acknowledged as sensor-shift optical image stabilization, with a seven-element lens and a focal pixel of 100%.

The iPhone 14 pro model also has a 12MP ultra-wide, with a focus of about 2.2 aperture, a six-element lens, and a focus pixel of 100%.

It also has a 2x and 3x telephoto camera using a 12MP camera, a varying focal range between 1.7 to 2.8 aperture, a 6x optical zoom range, and a digital zoom up to 15x.

Other prominent features include:

- The sapphire crystal lens cover.
- The photonic engine utilized the 48MP camera to produce brighter and more glamorous images.
- The deep fusion.
- The portrait mode with improved bokeh and deep control, and portrait lightning with six different effects.
- The night mode and night mode portrait, fostered by LiDAR Scanner.
- Macro photography.
- The Adaptive True Tone Flash.
- The Smart HDR 4.
- The Panorama: can take panoramic photos of up to 63 megapixels.
- The Photographic styles.

- The Apple ProRAW: gives proficient photographers the opening to merge and produce solid photos with the 48MP lens.
- Wide color capture for photos and Live photos.
- An ultra-wide Lens correction.
- An advanced red-eye correction.
- An auto image stabilization.
- Burst mode: whereby an iPhone camera captures striding objects and makes it possible to choose from an assortment of photos.
- Images are to be captured in a variety of file formats such as JPEG, HEIF, and DNG.

## The iPhone video recording features

With the help of the proRes and other iPhone video features, expert filmmakers can record videos ranging from 4k resolution at 24 frames to 30 frames, producing a standard cinematic video quality. There is also the chance of a continuous workflow with the help of DolbyVision HDR, making it possible to produce high-quality tapes and produce them more efficiently without interruption.

Filmmakers can also adjust their video speed from a  slow video interaction to a more timely video interaction.  They can also take a variety of still photos with an 8MP camera lens while still recording at a 4k resolution. Filmmakers can perform other tasks such as a continuous autofocus video technology system, audio and playback zoom, the 3x and 2x zoom adjustment, and record up to two or three different channels of songs into a single video setting. Videos are documented in a variety of formats such as the HEVC, the H264, and proRes.

## TrueDepth Camera Features

TrueDepth Camera Features include:

- 12MP camera

- $f$/1.9 aperture

- Autofocus with Focus Pixels

- Six-element lens

- Retina Flash

- Photonic Engine

- Deep Fusion

- Smart HDR 4

- Portrait mode with advanced bokeh and Depth Control

- Portrait Lighting with six effects (Natural, Studio, Contour, Stage, Stage Mono, High-Key Mono)

- Animoji and Memoji

- Night mode

- Photographic Styles

- Apple ProRAW

- Wide color capture for photos and Live Photos

- Lens correction

- Auto image stabilization

- Burst mode

- 4K video recording at 24 fps, 25 fps, 30 fps, or 60 fps

- 1080p HD video recording at 25 fps, 30 fps, or 60 fps

- Cinematic mode up to 4K HDR at 30 fps

- HDR video recording with Dolby Vision up to 4K at 60 fps

- ProRes video recording up to 4K at 30 fps (1080p at 30 fps for 128GB storage)

- Slo-mo video support for 1080p at 120 fps

- Time-lapse video with stabilization

- Night mode Time-lapse

- QuickTake video

- Cinematic video stabilization (4K, 1080p, and 720p)

Face ID is also enabled on the iPhone 14 series by TrueDepth camera for Facial Recognition.

## Relevant Camera Settings to Know

### How to enable 48MP ProRAW Photos

The ProRAW mode is a feature that allows you to take 48-megapixel pictures with the improved rear camera system. To enable ProRAW mode,

1.) Open Settings,

2.) Click on Camera

3.) And then select Formats and then choose Apple ProRaw and set the resolution to 48MP.

Once activated, there will be an icon labeled "RAW", visible in the upper right corner of the camera app. From there, you can easily toggle the ProRAW mode on or off.

Since ProRAW images have a 48-megapixel resolution, they often have more detail and can allow for flexible editing. At the same time, these 48-megapixel images are large files which can take up to 75MB or more for a single picture, so it is prudent to consider your device's storage space when you want to use this feature.

## Enable 4K Cinematic Mode

The Cinematic mode allows videos to be recorded in 4K. To activate this feature,

1.) Open Settings,

2.) Click on Camera

3.) And then select Record Cinematic.

4.) Next, choose between recording 4K videos at 30 frames per second or 4K videos at 24 frames per second.

Since the iPhone 13 was released, the cinematic mode has a depth effect with automatic focus changes for "cinema-style" videos.

## How to Optimize Action Mode for Lower Light

The Action Mode feature available on the iPhone 14 models, allow a smoother looking video by adjusting to motion significant shakes and vibrations. This feature comes in handy in recording a video of a runner, filming while off-roading in a vehicle, etc.

To activate this feature, simply launch the Camera app and click on the Action mode icon at the upper left corner for video. Also, you can optimize the Action mode for lower-light conditions by,

> 1.) Opening Settings,

> 2.) Click on Camera

> 3.) And then select Record Video.

> 4.) Next, toggle the Action Mode Lower Light option on or off.

## How to Turn on a Startup Sound

This feature essentially enables users to play a sound anytime the device is powered off or powered on. To enable this feature,

> 1.) Open Settings,

2.) Click on Accessibility

3.) And then select Audio/Visual.

4.) Next, choose Power On & Off Sounds.

## How to Adjust Advanced Camera Settings on iPhone

With Advanced Camera features, it is possible to take pictures more rapidly, look at scenes not within the camera frame, and apply customized and improved looks to your pictures.

## How to Toggle View Outside the Frame on and Off

On iPhone 11 and later models (including the iPhone 14), the camera shows in the preview pane, a part of the scene that is not within the frame but can be captured with another lens in the camera system that has a wider field of view.

To toggle this display off:

1.) Open Settings,

2.) Click on Camera,

3.) And then switch off View Outside the Frame.

## How to Turn Prioritize Faster Shooting on or off

From iPhone X models and later models, it is possible to adjust how images are processed via the Prioritize Faster Shooting setting. This allows you to take more pictures by quickly tapping the Shutter button.

This feature is activated by default. To deactivate this feature,

1.) Open Settings,

2.) Click on Camera,

3.) And then switch off Prioritize Faster Shooting.

## How to Toggle Lens Correction on and Off

On iPhone 12 and later models (including the iPhone 14), it is possible to give pictures taken with the front camera or Ultra-wide camera a more natural look via the Lens Correction setting. This feature is activated by default. To deactivate it,

1.) Open Settings,

2.) Click on Camera,

3.) And then switch off Lens Correction.

## Toggle Scene Detection on or off

Via the scene detection feature, it is possible to identify the scene in the preview pane and apply an appropriate look that highlights the best qualities of the scene.

This feature is activated by default. To deactivate it,

    1.)  Open Settings,

    2.)  Click on Camera,

    3.)    And then switch off Lens Correction

# Capturing Photos on the iPhone 14 Pro

The iPhone 14 Pro is saddled with an impressive Camera System and Camera App. This combination is a popular recipe for great photos. The three cameras behind the iPhone 14 Pro and the iPhone 14 Pro Max –48MP Main Camera, 12MP Ultra-wide Camera, and the 12MP Telephoto Lens– makes this possible. Below are different ways to take pictures with the iPhone 14:

## Via the Shutter Button

Conventionally this is the popular way to take photos with the iPhone as well as any other smartphone. To use this method of picture taking,

1.) Launch the Camera app and
2.) Fit the subject within the Camera preview pane,
3.) Then click on the circular Shutter icon visible at the bottom middle part of the screen.

## Via the Volume Buttons

Asides from using the popular shutter icon, you can also take pictures with the volume buttons. This method is generally ideal because it prevents touching the screen and altering the focus on the subject in the preview pane. This feature is activated by default on the Apple iPhone 14. This means that you can launch the Camera app and once you have your subject in view, you can just as easily press the volume up button or down button as you would tap the shutter icon. This would capture a photo.

Pressing and holding down the volume button will begin recording a video. Once you release the volume button, the video recording will stop and be saved to your Photos.

You can change what happens when you press and hold down the volume button from recording a video to taking burst photos. To do this,

1.) Open Settings,
2.) Click on Camera,
3.) And then switch off or on burst capture

## Via Apple QuickTake

Apple QuickTake makes it possible to snap pictures, record videos and take burst photos seamlessly. When you touch the Shutter icon, you will take a picture. Tapping and holding the shutter icon will record a video instantly without having to go to video mode. Just like with the volume button, the video will continue to be captured as long as you hold down your finger on the shutter icon. Lifting your finger stops the video recording. If you want to record a video hands-free, simply slide the shutter icon to the right. This locks the video mode and you can raise your finger without stopping the video recording.

To take burst photos via the Apple QuickTake mode, tap the shutter icon and then, slide it quickly to the left. As long as you hold the shutter icon in that position, the camera will capture burst photos. While the burst photos are being taken, a counter will be visible at the original location of the shutter icon indicating how many shots have been taken.

## The iPhone 14 Camera Modes

The iPhone 14 has several different camera modes for shooting different scenes. These modes include:

**Macro Mode**: The macro mode is useful for taking detailed, up-close photos of a subject. To shoot in macro mode, simply move the camera really close to the subject and then the Macro Mode will automatically switch on. With the subject within a few millimeters away from the lens, the macro mode can still focus on it. To deactivate the automatic activation of the macro mode, open Settings, Tap Camera and then toggle off automatic macro mode.

**Night Mode**: The iPhone 14 Pro also has the Night mode that is useful for taking clear pictures in the dark/night. In this mode, the camera simulates the impact of a slow shutter speed and adjusts the shutter duration based on how much the phone and subject move. This way, the camera shutter does not close as quickly as it normally would, thereby allowing more light to reach the sensor and take clear photos in low-light or dim scenarios.

While holding the phone in your hands, the camera shutter may stay open for about two or three seconds. On a tripod, the iPhone may limit it to about 30 seconds. You can adjust how long the shutter stays open by clicking on Night Mode and moving the slider left or right. The options for a 10, 15, or 30 second shutter delay may not be available if the device is moving too much.

**Portrait Mode**: The portrait mode is great for taking pictures that focus solely on the subject while blurring out other objects within the frame as well as the background. To use this feature, simply bring the subject within the frame, portrait mode will then be highlighted at the bottom of the screen and options will be available to manage the portrait mode. There are a number of filters to switch between such as the contour light, stage light, stage light mono, etc.

**Cinematic Mode:** The cinematic mode makes use of the depth of field effect and maintains the subject within the frame in a way that keeps it sharp and blurring the background and foreground.

**Video Mode**: This mode is essentially responsible for creating video recordings.

**Time-lapse Mode**: This mode is used for creating a time-lapse video of motion over a period

**Slo-mo**: This camera mode uses the slow-motion effect for video recordings, making them play slower than they normally would for dramatic effect.

**Pano mode**: This camera mode is essential for capturing a panoramic landscape or other scene.

**Square mode**: This camera mode focuses on using app-friendly picture sizes when shooting. There's the option of choosing between 4:3, 16:9 and other aspect ratios.

## How to Switch Between the Lenses

As already discussed in previous chapters, the iPhone 14 comes with three different lenses that serve quite different purposes. Switching between these lenses for seamless shooting is pretty easy.

Switching between the Standard Wide-Angle Lens, Ultra-Wide-Angle Lens and the Telephoto Lens

To switch between the standard wide-angle lens, ultra-wide angle and telephoto lens,

1. Launch the Camera app
2. While in Photo mode, choose between the unique lenses available on the iPhone 14 by clicking on the numbered buttons visible at the lower part of the viewfinder.

   .5 represents the Ultra-wide lens

   1x is the standard Wide-angle lens

   While 2 represents the Telephoto lens.

## Fine Tuning the Zoom in and Out

The Zoom feature helps to take a closer view of subjects while shooting.

Generally, using this feature is just as easy as pinching in and out on the subject within the frame in the Camera app. However, with the iPhone 14, it is also possible to have a more precise navigation and control of the zoom levels 0.5x, 1x, 2x, 2.5x, and 3x. This is done by simply touching and holding the zoom controls. A slider will then appear, with which you can drag left or right till you achieve your desired zoom level.

## Scanning QR Codes

Scanning QR codes help to avoid memorizing unnecessary URLs or even having to input them to visit a website. Via a QR code, it is easy to scan and visit a website directly from the Camera App.

To do this,

1.) Launch the Camera app
2.) Switch to the rear camera and position the QR code within the frame
3.) Next, touch the notification to visit the link associated with the QR code.

## Mirroring Front Camera

On the iPhone 14, it is possible to take mirrored selfies that capture selfies exactly as they appear in the camera viewfinder.

To activate this feature,

1. Launch Settings,

2. Select Camera and then

3. Proceed to switch on Mirror Front Camera

# Manipulating Images on iPhone 14

On the iPhone 14, it is possible to tweak and adjust images to highlight their best features or add more beauty to them. The iPhone 14 provides several tools for photo editing.

## Editing a Photo or Video

Once a picture has been taken, it is pretty easy to edit it via the Photos app. Adjusting the light and color, image rotating, filter addition, image cropping, etc., are few of the many edits you can make to a picture. It is also possible to go back to the original photo looks after the editing.

With iCloud Photos, edited pictures and videos are stored across all devices with the iCloud.

## How to Adjust light and color of an image

To adjust the light and color of an image:

1. Launch Photos and select a video thumbnail or picture to open it in full screen.
2. Tap on Edit and swipe leftward below the picture to reveal the effects you can edit in the picture. Available effects include Brilliance, Exposure, Shadows, and Exposure.

3. Pick your desired effect and move your finger along the slider to set it. There is an outline around the button that shows the level of adjustments you have set for each effect.

4. Click on Done to save edits or click on Cancel and then Discard Changes if you aren't satisfied with your edits and don't wish to save them.

Tapping the effects icon is one way to automatically edit videos or pictures with effects.

# How to Apply Filter Effects

1.) Launch Photos and select a video thumbnail or picture to open it in full screen.

2.) Tap on Edit and then select ⊗choose between Vivid, Dramatic or Silvertone to apply these filters.

3.) Pick your desired filter and move your finger along the slider to set it. Tap the picture you're editing to compare its original look

4.) Click on Done to save edits or click on Cancel and then Discard Changes if you aren't satisfied with your edits and don't wish to save them.

# Copy and Paste Edits to Multiple Photos

Just as easily, it is possible to replicate edits made on one picture on another picture or a batch of photos, all at ones.

To do this,

1.) Open the edited images whose edits you want to copy.

2.) Click on the three horizontal dots ⊙ for options and then select Copy Edits.

3.) Click on ❮ to open the photo library.

4.) Next, touch Select and pick the picture or pictures that you want to paste the edits onto by tapping their thumbnails.

Alternatively, you can open a picture or video and then select Paste Edits from the options menu⊙.

## How to Write or draw on a picture

To write or draw on a picture, first open it in Photos by clicking on its thumbnail to open it in full screen.

1.) Click on Edit and then touch the Draw icon Ⓐ.

2.) Using the different drawing tools and colors available, draw on the picture. You can click on ⊕ to include a caption, shapes, text, signature or magnify the picture.

3.) Click on Done to save edits or click on Cancel and then Discard Changes if you aren't satisfied with your edits and don't wish to save them.

# Before and After Effects of Photo Edits

If you want to compare the edited picture with the original picture, simply tap on the photo while editing.

## Undo or redo edits

You can undo previous edits or redo edits by touching the ⟲ and ⟳ icons respectively. These icons are located at the top of the screen.

# Different Cropping Options

For picture cropping,

1.) Launch Photos and select a video thumbnail or picture to open it in full screen.

2.) Click on Edit and then select ⬦

3.) Next, proceed with either of the following options:

- **Crop manually**: Do this by moving the rectangle corners to the include just the area you want to keep in your final image. Alternatively, you can pinch the photo in or out to position your desired parts in the crop rectangle.

- **Crop to a standard preset ratio**: Click on

and then select a crop aspect ratio such as 16:9, square or 5:4.

- **Rotate**: Rotate the picture 90 degrees by clicking on .

- **Flip**: Flip the image horizontally by clicking on .

4.) Click on Done to save edits or click on Cancel and then Discard Changes if you aren't satisfied with your edits and don't wish to save them.

# How to Straighten and Adjust Perspective

To straighten and adjust perspective,

- Launch Photos and select a video thumbnail or picture to open it in full screen.

- Click on Edit and then select ⌗.

- Next, swipe leftward below the picture to reveal the effects you can edit: Horizontal, Vertical or Straighten.

- Pick your desired effect you wish to edit and move your finger along the slider to set it. There is an outline around the button that shows the level of adjustments you have set for each effect.

- Click on Done to save edits or click on Cancel and then Discard

Changes if you aren't satisfied with your edits and don't wish to save them.

## Using Filters Correctly

Using a filter is pretty easy. It gives your photos a beautiful color effect.

To use a filter for your pictures,

1.) Launch the camera and select either the photo or Portrait mode.

2.) Next, click on the ⌃ icon and then select ⊛.

3.) Filters will then be visible at the bottom of the screen below the viewer. Swipe left or right to preview them and then make your pick.

## Reverting to an Original Photo or Video

Once an edit is completed and your changes saved, you can still revert to the original image or video. To to this,

1.  Open the edited picture or video and then open the list of options by tapping on the three horizontal dots .

2.  Next, select Revert to Original.

# Changing the Aspect Ratio

To change the aspect ratio when editing,

1.) Launch Photos and select a video thumbnail or picture to open it in full screen.

2.) Click on Edit and then select ⊕

3.) Next, proceed with **Crop to a standard preset ratio**. Click on ▧ and then select a crop aspect ratio such as 16:9, square or 5:4.

4.) Click on Done to save edits or click on Cancel and then Discard Changes if you aren't satisfied with your edits and don't wish to save them.

# Indicator for Camera Rolling

A timer or indicator is a great way to announce a shot or get a pose ready for it. To set a timer on the iPhone 14 camera,

1.) Launch the camera and click on .

2.) Next click on and then set the timer duration to either 3 seconds, 10 seconds, etc.

3.) Finally, start the timer by tapping the shutter button.

# Additional Controls on The Camera App

## Learn to Take Great Selfies

The front cameras on the phone are selfie-dedicated. This way, you can still take great pictures yourself without having another person do it for you.

**Taking a Selfie**

To take a selfie:

Launch the Camera and tap on to switch to the front camera and then position your face within the frame and press the Shutter button or the volume button to capture the selfie.

## Switching Between Close and Wide-Angle Selfies

To have a closer or wider view for your selfies on the iPhone 14. Simply, touch the arrows within the frame. This increases the field of view. You can also decrease the field of view the same way.

## Utilizing the Night Mode

The night mode is a great feature that allows you to take pictures in dim or lowly-lit scenarios.

The icon turning yellow indicates that the Night mode is on. Touch the Shutter button and the steadily hold your phone in position to take the shot.

If you want to experiment with the Night mode, tap the ⊜ icon and then drag the slider to set your preferred exposure time.

With the iPhone 14, Night mode is available with the front camera and when you switch between 0.5x, 1x, 2x, 2.5x, or 3x.

## Having Fun with Live Photos

Live photos are a better way to make memories with your pictures. The Live Photo picture takes a video and audio recording of what happens right before and right after a picture is taken. The best part is that taking a Live Photo is just as seamless as taking a regular picture.

## Taking a Live Photo

**To take a Live Photo:**

1.) Launch the Camera and ensure that it is set at Photo Mode and Live Photo is turned on. The icon at the top of the screen indicates that Live Photo is turned on. Live Photo is turned off when the icon has a slash right through it. Touch the icon to activate or deactivate Live Photo.

2.) Touch the Camera Shutter button to capture a Live Photo

3.) To play the Live Photo, touch the photo thumbnail at the screen's bottom. To play it, touch and hold the screen.

## Editing a Live Photo

Editing a Live Photo provides the opportunity to change its key photo and include key effects such as Loop and Bounce.

**To Edit Live Photos**

You can also add filters, crop the picture, trim the length, mute the sound of a Live Photo. To do this,

1.) Open the Live Photo and select Edit.

2.) Touch the Live Photo icon and choose to either:

Set a key photo: Drag the white frame on the frame viewer to your preferred picture and touch Make Key Photo. Then, click Done.

Trim a Live Photo: Move either end of the frame viewer and deciding which frames the Live Photo plays.

Make a still photo: Click on the Live Photo button to Turn off the Live Photo feature. This makes the Live Photo a still picture of its key photo.

Mute a Live Photo: To mute a Live Photo, touch the sound icon 🔊 at the screen top. Unmute it using the same technique.

## Viewing a Live Photo

To play a Live Photo, simply touch the Photo thumbnail at the screen's bottom. Then touch and hold the screen to play it.

## How to View Custom Effects of a Live Photo

It is possible to add and view personalized effects on a Live Photo. Added effects to Live Photos can make them fun videos. To do this,

Open the Live Photo

Click on the Live Photo icon at the top left corner and select either:

Live: This setting applies the Live video playback feature.

Loop: This setting repeats the action in the Live Video in a continuous looping video.

Bounce: This setting rewinds the action in the Live Photo backward and forward.

Long Exposure: This setting simulates a DSLR-like ling exposure effect by blurring motion.

Off: This feature turns off the Live video playback feature or applied effect.

## Slow Motion Video

A slow motion video typically has its action slowed down by a special effect so, the viewer can get a clear and dramatic feel of the entire action.

## Recording a Slow-motion Video

Recording a slow-motion video using the Slo-Mo mode happens just as like a regular video is recorded. However, you see the slow-motion effect only during the video playback.

It's also possible to choose what part of the video has the slow-motion effect and what part doesn't.

To record a slow-motion video,

1.) Launch the camera and then choose Slo-Mo mode. With the iPhone 14, it is possible to use the front camera to record in Slo-Mo Mode

2.) Begin recording by touching the Record button or by pressing the volume button.

Pressing the Camera Shutter button while recording will capture a still photo.

3.) Finish recording by touching the Record button or by pressing the volume button.

If you want to set a specific part of the video to play in slow motion,

1.) Touch the video thumbnail and then, select Edit.
2.) Drag the vertical bars at the bottom of the frame viewer to pick what parts of the video you want to play back in slow motion.

It is also possible to change the resolution and frame rate of slow motion video. To change the slow-motion recording settings,

1.) Launch Settings and then select Camera.
2.) Click on Record Slo-mo

Alternatively, you can use quick toggles to change the frame rate and video resolution while recording.

## How to Lock Camera Focus and Exposure

The iPhone 14's Camera uses focus to fixate on a specified area within the frame. By default, the iPhone camera automatically sets its focus and exposure, then uses the face detection feature to balance the exposure across many faces. It is also possible to manually set the focus and exposure:

To do this,

1.) Launch the Camera
2.) Touch the screen to see the automatic Focus area and exposure setting.
3.) Next, choose where you would like to move the focus area to, by touching there.
4.) Then, slide your finger up and down the exposure slider ☀ to set the exposure.
5.) Lock the manual focus and exposure settings for subsequent shots, touch and hold the focus area until you see AE/AF Lock.

To unlock the focus and exposure settings, touch the screen.

On the iPhone 14 Pro, you can fix and lock the exposure settings for subsequent pictures. Touch the ⬤ icon and then click on the ⊕ icon. Drag the slider along to set exposure. The exposure remains locked until the next time the Camera application is opened.

Visit Settings and click on Camera, then select Preserve Settings and turn on Exposure Adjustment.

## Having Fun with your iPhone 14

Memojis are a fun way to create, share and have fun with your iPhone 14. You can design your own customized Memoji —select tone, skin, glasses, headwear and more. It's also possible to design different Memoji for different moods.

# How to Create your own Memoji

To design or create a Memoji,

1. Select 🐷 in a conversation and then choose +.
2. Touch specific features and pick the option you want for yourMemoji. As you add more features, the Memoji comes alive.
3. Touch Done to include the Memoji you created in your collection.

If you want to edit, delete or duplicate a memoji, click on 🐷, select the memoji and then open the list of options by tapping ⋯

# Sending Animated or Memoji Recordings

In conversations, iMessage makes sticker packs automatically depending on your Memoji and Memoji Characters. It is possible to use stickers to show a number of emotions in novel ways. For this,

1.) Select in a conversation.
2.) Touch the Memoji in the upper row to see the stickers in the pack.
3.) Send a sticker by doing any of the following:

Tap the sticker and add it to the message bubble. Include a comment if you prefer, then touch to send.

Tap and hold down a sticker and drag it on top of the message in the conversation. The sticker will be sent automatically when you add it to the message.

# Configuring Other Camera Settings

## The Portrait Mode on iPhone 14

The iPhone 14 supports the Portrait mode. This means that when taking pictures, you can use a depth-of-field effect to keep your subject in the frame sharp while creating a beautifully blurred background and foreground. Subjects can either be pets, people, objects, etc.

It is also possible to include and adjust various lighting effects to pictures you take in portrait mode on the iPhone 14. Selfies, as well, can be taken with the front camera in portrait mode.

## Adjusting Portrait Photos

You can apply professional-looking lighting effects to pictures you take in Portrait mode.

To do this, launch the camera and choose Portrait mode.

1. From the visible instructions on the screen, frame your subject into the yellow portrait box.

2. Next, move    to pick a lighting effect. You can choose between

Natural Light, Studio Light, Contour Light, Stage Light, Stage Light Mono, High-key Light.

3. Touch the Camera Shutter button to capture your picture.

## How Not to Include the Blur

After taking a portrait shot, you can also choose whether you want the portrait mode effect to remain in the picture or you want to remove it. To remove the portrait mode effect,

1.) Open the Photos app and then select the portrait photo.

2.) Next, touch the Edit button and select Portrait to toggle the effect off or on.

## Low-light Photos with Night Mode on iPhone 14

On the iPhone 14 Pro and iPhone 14 Pro Max, the Night mode turns on when you take a Portrait Mode picture in low-light conditions with the wide (1x) lens.

# Getting the Most of Your iPhone 14

## Best Practices for Smartphone Photography

Since smartphones in general began creating devices with impressive camera ranges, smartphone photography has become a thing. However, not everyone is conversant with the possibilities a smartphone could deliver or what measures to take in getting the best photos with a smartphone's camera.

Below are 10 tips and tricks for better smartphone photography:

1.) **Use a good camera:** A good camera is more often than not, a foundation for great photography.

Thanks to advancements in technology, there's so many improvements and possibilities with smartphone cameras. You can start off your journey to professional smartphone photography with a good camera. The Apple iPhone 14's camera ticks all the boxes on qualities of a good camera. Smartphone products from Google Pixel, OnePlus, Samsung Galaxy, etc. As such, bagging one of those devices would do a great deal in improving your photography.

2.) **Go for the best lighting possible:** Lighting plays a major role in taking great shots. Whether natural or artificial, adequate lighting produces brighter subjects and this would equate to better pictures. When it comes to smartphone photography, natural light is usually preferred by most smartphone photographers, especially for outdoor shooting. However, as long as the right exposure and focus settings are in place, there's so much that can be done with natural lighting.

**3.) Adjust your focus and exposure**

Knowing how to manage the amount of light hits the shutter when taking a picture goes a long way to determine how your final image will turn out. Ideally, the exposure is supposed to be adjusted as much as the scenery which you're shooting changes.

When it comes to Focus, it is best to manually set the focus on the subject. Shooting busy scenes can be distracting, especially for smartphone cameras that have auto focus switched on. This can make the final image appear blurry.

4.) **Use the burst feature more often**: The burst feature rapidly takes shots as long as your finger is on the shutter button. This feature is great for scenes with a lot of moving parts. This way, you can't miss taking a shot. For the best photos with burst mode, it is best to take lock focus and exposure.

5.) **Utilize the camera grid**: One of the qualities of good pictures is proper positioning and the camera grid helps the photographer to achieve this. The camera grid segments the camera frame into nine parts. This makes it easy to position the subject vertically and horizontally within the frame.

6.) **Learn more about your camera's features**: A good photographer should be able to navigate through a device's camera, utilizing all of its features efficiently. Being able to do this is only possible when the photographer knows all there is to know about the devices features and functions.

7.) **Use a microphone for video recordings**: Generally, smartphones use the device's in-built camera as its microphone to record sound while the camera records video. This method of recording sound can be quite inefficient in some situations. As such, it is best to utilize an external microphone that is specialized in recording audio efficiently and can be attached to the subject during video recordings.

8.) **Try add-on lens**: Add-on lenses are great for making the most out of a device's camera. They produce better photos with more detail, improved zoom and a range of other features. Including an add-on lens to your photography tools collection can improve your photography even better.

9.) **Hold steady when shooting**: Holding steady is an essential part of recording videos and audio. This helps you to get a better view of your subjects and avoid blurry photos. Certain features such as Night Mode also require you to hold steady for better results.

10.) **Photo Editing does more than you think**: A larger number of pictures you find online have been edited. Editing plays a major role in enhancing and improving the final result of a shot. There is only so much a camera can give in a raw picture, however with editing, there's a ton of other effects and designs that could be added to a picture. Hence, adding photo editing skills to your photography skills will do more in improving your photography.

# iPhone 14 Videography

## Video Quality

The video quality is usually determined by a combination of different factors including the frames per second (fps), video resolution settings. The iPhone 14 camera, by default, records videos at 30 frames per second (fps). This frame rate produces standard quality videos, however, the iPhone 14 also allows you to pick other frame rates and video resolution settings.

It's important to consider available storage when augmenting video quality. This is because higher quality videos will faster frame rates and higher resolutions equate to larger video file size.

It's possible to easily change the video resolution and frame rates using the quick toggles visible right on the camera screen. You can do this on the iPhone 14 by locating the quick toggles at the top-right corner to switch between HD or 4k recording and 24, 25, 30, or 60 frames per second in Video mode.

## How to Shoot Videos with Your iPhone 14

The iPhone camera can record videos and QuickTake videos. To record a video with the iPhone 14 camera,

1.) Launch the Camera app and then switch to Video mode.
2.) To begin recording, touch the Record button or press any of the

volume keys. It is possible to perform any of the following actions while recording:

**Take a still photo**: Pressing the white shutter button while recording will take a still photo.

**Zoom in or out**: The zoom feature can be utilized for a closer look by pinching the screen.

**Use a more precise zoom**: Touching and holding down 1x and then dragging the slider to the left will present a more precise zoom control.

3.) To stop recording, touch the Record button or press any of the volume keys.

# Professional iPhone 14 Videos

The iPhone 14 Pro and iPhone 14 Pro Max make it possible to record and edit videos professional videos in ProRes that guarantees higher color fidelity and less compression.

The ProRes feature is available on both front and rear cameras. Professional videos recorded in this mode typically have larger file sizes.

To set up ProRes,

1.) Launch Settings
2.) Select Camera
3.) Next, click on Formats and switch on Apple ProRes

To record a professional video with the ProRes feature,

1.) Launch the Camera app and then switch to Video mode.

2.) Next, click on the ProRes icon to switch it on.

3.) To begin recording, touch the Record button or press any of the volume keys.

4.) To stop recording, touch the Record button or press any of the volume keys.

5.) Click on the ProRes icon anytime you want to turn the ProRes mode off.

# Third Party Camera Apps

Below is a list of third-party camera apps that will help you make the most out of your iPhone 14 camera.

1.) **Halide Mark II**: The Halide Mark II is among the best pure-photography applications available in the market. Famous for its won award in 2022 —Apple Design Awards—, the Halide Mark II is a great app that provides a wholesome method of controlling and utilizing the iPhone's Camera.

Features of the app worth noting include the manual focus that has the Focus Peaking and Focus Lupe. These systems ensure that the relevant aspects of focus are provided within the app. With the app, the user also has the ability to manually manage exposure with shutter speed, ISO, and white balance settings. The grid overlay available on the app also has a built-in leveling notification that ensures the image is as level as possible.

The Halide Mark II also makes available color zebra stripes, histograms and Extended Dynamic Range 14-bit RAW streaming waveform views for users who have more demanding needs.

Great for iPhone cameras with a depth-of-field sensors like the TrueDepth camera, the Halide Mark II provides access to a visualizer that assesses the depth of different elements in a picture before taking the shot. Users are also able to control the level of depth effect in a picture with the app. It also has a RAW and ProRAW support and instant development.

2.) **ProCamera**: The ProCamera is another ideal third-party camera application. With an overly simple interface, the ProCamera helps photographers to seamlessly handle rapid shots as well as carefully planned shots. The automatic settings are great and would produce breathtaking pictures but there's a number of other functions and options to explore.

The ProCamera offers manual and semi-automatic modes that feature a manual focus with focus peaking, live histograms, manual white balance control, exposure compensation with Zebra Stripes, and a portrait mode with a depth of preview of bokeh-based images.

Also supports RAW, TIFF, ProRAW, JPG and HEIF. The ProCamera does not only work with pictures. For videos, as well, the ProCamera can handle up to 4K HDR videos, continuous video focus, complete with manual controls, support for Bluetooth, USB and Lightning microphones and high bitrate recording.

Making it a complete photography package, the ProCamera also offers editing tools for pictures taken.

3.) **Adobe Lightroom**: The Adobe Lightroom is another popular photography app for editing pictures, as well as Photoshop. The smartphone version of the Adobe Lightroom offers more versatility as it offers camera controls and can be used to take pictures as a third-party camera app.

As a camera app, the Adobe Lightroom functions in three major categories. These categories include: the Automatic category that offers an easy-to-navigate shooting experience, the

Professional and the High Dynamic Range that offers more details controls for picture taking.

Manual controls available on the Adobe Lightroom app for photography include exposure compensation, ISO, white balance, managing focus, exposure time, etc.

Grid settings, aspect ratio options, a timer exposure lock and highlight clipping warnings are additional options for more control on the Adobe Lightroom.

The app also features a high-level editing system that provides several presets which the picture can be reviewed in before shooting.

After snapping, the pictures become available for editing in the Lightroom experience.

4.) **VSCO**: VSCO is another third-party camera app that offers even more filters and presets. Also known for editing, the VSCO fits a camera capability right under its numerous features. Although, its camera features are not exactly up to par with other third-party cameras, it makes up for this lapse in post-processing of photos.

When it comes to picture editing with VSCO, the level of improvement and transformation it can give a picture is as a result of the numerous presets available on the app.

# Caring for your iPhone Camera

Your iPhone Camera is one of the most high-value hardware components of your phone. As such, caring for your iPhone camera is an ideal way to preserve and extend the longevity of your device.

Below are several ways by which you can take proper care of your iPhone camera:

1. **Cleaning with a microfiber cloth**: A microfiber cloth typically has little to no debris, as such, your camera lens and device screen would not risk being scratched while cleaning. Compressed air is usually an alternative for cleaning your iPhone camera and screen.

However, in situations where dust resides underneath the lens or the lens is damaged while cleaning, the device would need an expert to handle its repair.

2. **Avoid using chemical products for cleaning**: As you may already know, chemical cleaning products may have unsavory effects on your camera lens ranging from discoloration to an unhealthy lens reaction depending on the chemical product. Hence, it is best to use water or other specified camera and phone cleaning product.

3. **Have a protective case for your phone:** Having a phone case does more wonders for your iPhone camera and screen than you may imagine. Most phone

cases have an extra protective layer that covers the camera when not in use. These type of phone cases shield the camera lens from external debris or elements that may affect the camera performance.

4. **Always place the phone on a soft base:** Consciously picking only the soft surfaces to place your iPhone is a great way to care for your phone. Hard or rough surfaces can significantly damage your iPhone camera and screen within a short period of time. As a rule of thumb, carry around a soft piece of cloth or tissue alongside your phone to create a soft base for your phone. This would prevent the camera

lens module from coming in direct contact with the rough surface.

5. **Store the phone in a different pouch or pocket**: Putting the phone in the same pouch or bag with other items such as pens, keys, pins, chargers, exposes the phone to risks of getting damages. From scratches to breakages, the damages the device is exposed to in such spaces can be aggravated especially when the bag is in continuous uneven motion. One way to avoid these damages is to have a separate pouch or pocket for storing your phone.

# Conclusion

Apple's newest launch, an evolution of the iPhone 13 series, has proven to be the most remarkable smartphone released in the iPhone system today.

The new iPhone 14 pro models, which come in four gorgeous colors, have been furnished with improvements and offer high proficiency physical features and power settings. It introduces a new outstanding feature called the dynamic Island, which is highly adaptive and can fluidly expand as you interact with your iPhone.

The iPhone 14 pro model has also been compacted with other dispositions, ranging from small components like the ceramic shield layer to high-enhancing elements like the camera features and other technological specifications.

With the level of refinement found in the digital world and information technology, Apple has proven, yet again, to be one of the best multinational corporations when it comes to smartphones and other gadgets. It has also raised the bar in the digital world with the recent release of the iPhone 14 pro model and, perhaps, not only intends to retain that title but also, to expand to become more between the other smartphone collaborations and the digital world at large.

Made in the USA
Coppell, TX
02 July 2023

18684424R30072